Christmas Quirky Jokes ii

Tammy M. Shoemate
(Grammy Tammy)

NEWMAN SPRINGS PUBLISHING
320 Broad Street
Red Bank, NJ 07701

First originally published by Newman Springs Publishing 2021

ISBN 978-1-63692-482-3 (Paperback)
ISBN 978-1-63692-483-0 (Digital)

Printed in the United States of America

To my family—Kevin, Dalton,
Briana, and Logan
And to Jesus, my Savior

Why did Santa try to prevent the tooth fairy from coming into his room? Because he was worried she would take his sweet tooth from him.

Why was Santa anxious to bring the tree he cut down back to Mrs. Claus? Because he was sitting on pines and needles.

Why did Comet the reindeer strap a rocket on his back so he could shoot for the stars? Because he wanted a Missle Tow if he got tired.

What is Santa's favorite dance? The peppermint twist.

Why did Santa invite the woodland animals to live in his Christmas tree? Because Mrs. Claus requested he get a fir tree to decorate.

Why did Santa want to take a tropical vacation alone after delivering presents? He wanted a blue Christmas without you.

What did Rudolph tell Santa when he was finished pulling his sleigh from a night of delivering presents? "The buck stops here."

What did the polar bear say to Santa as she was giving him a bear hug because he gave her a present? "Grin and bear it."

What do you get when you combine an elf and a sugar plum? A little bit of sweet relief.

What happened to Rudolph when he heard the other reindeer talking about him? He was seeing red.

Why did Santa want to increase production in his workshop? Because the elves were coming in short.

What happens to Santa's reindeer when they are no longer able to pull his sleigh in the air? They have to learn to hoof it.

About the Author

Tammy works as a nurse and is a firm believer that laughter is the best medicine. She sees the evidence with the people she takes care of at the facility where she works. Many of the staff and residents look forward to and enjoy the joke of the day. It is Tammy's desire to bring joy to those around her by tickling their giggles. Laughter is a great tool that she is able to incorporate to give back to those who need to laugh the most.

Why did Santa try to prevent the tooth fairy from coming into his room? Because he was worried she would take his sweet tooth from him.

Why did Santa try to prevent the tooth fairy from coming into his room? Because he was worried she would take his sweet tooth from him.

Why did Santa try to prevent the tooth fairy from coming into his room? Because he was worried she would take his sweet tooth from him.

Why did Santa try to prevent the tooth fairy from coming into his room? Because he was worried she would take his sweet tooth from him.

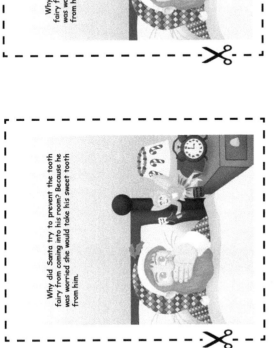

Why did Santa try to prevent the tooth fairy from coming into his room? Because he was worried she would take his sweet tooth from him.

Why did Santa try to prevent the tooth fairy from coming into his room? Because he was worried she would take his sweet tooth from him.

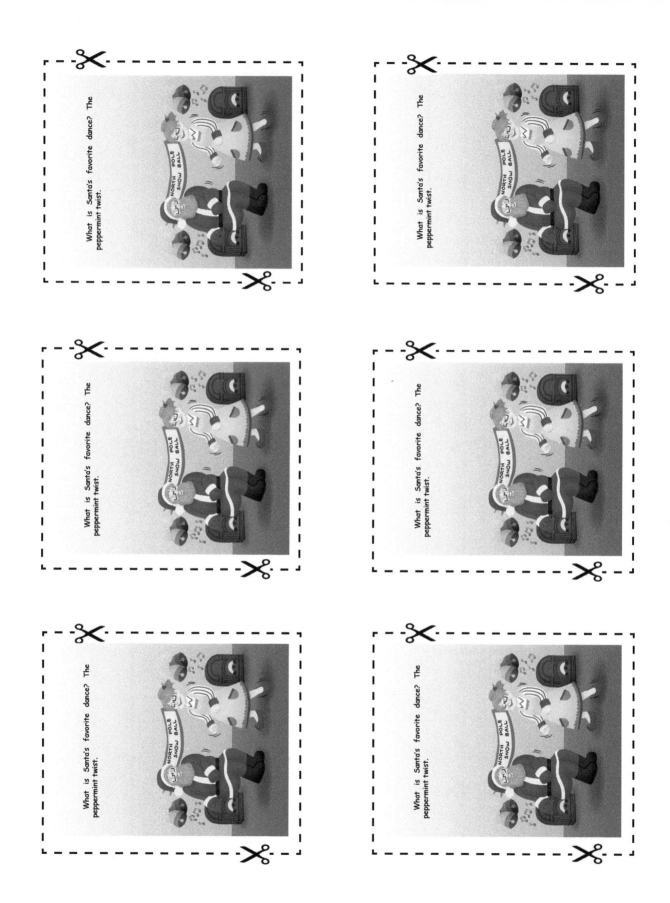

Why did Santa invite the woodland animals to live in his Christmas tree? Because Mrs. Claus requested he get a fir tree to decorate.

Why did Santa invite the woodland animals to live in his Christmas tree? Because Mrs. Claus requested he get a fir tree to decorate.

Why did Santa invite the woodland animals to live in his Christmas tree? Because Mrs. Claus requested he get a fir tree to decorate.

Why did Santa invite the woodland animals to live in his Christmas tree? Because Mrs. Claus requested he get a fir tree to decorate.

Why did Santa invite the woodland animals to live in his Christmas tree? Because Mrs. Claus requested he get a fir tree to decorate.

Why did Santa invite the woodland animals to live in his Christmas tree? Because Mrs. Claus requested he get a fir tree to decorate.

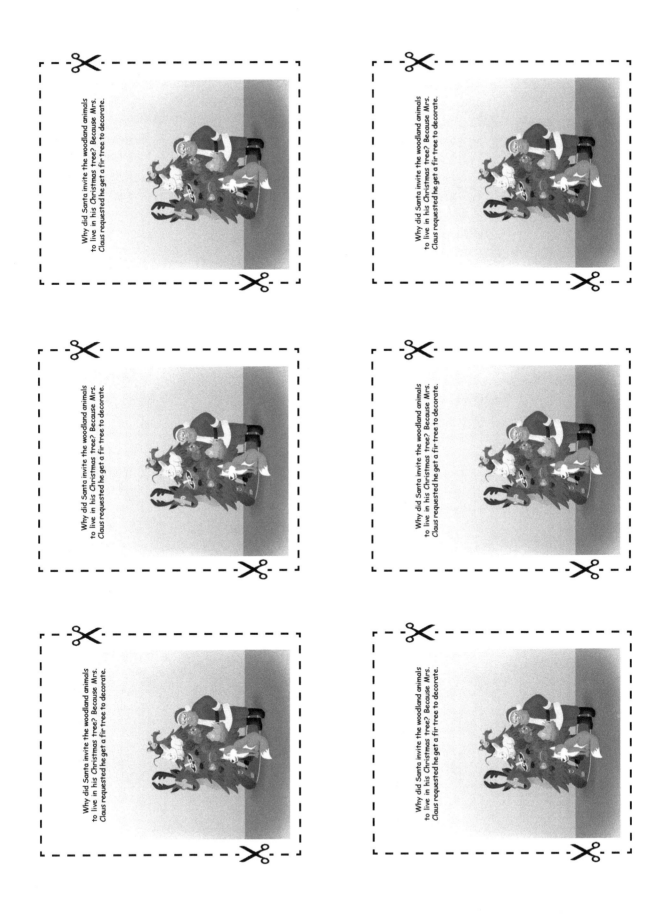

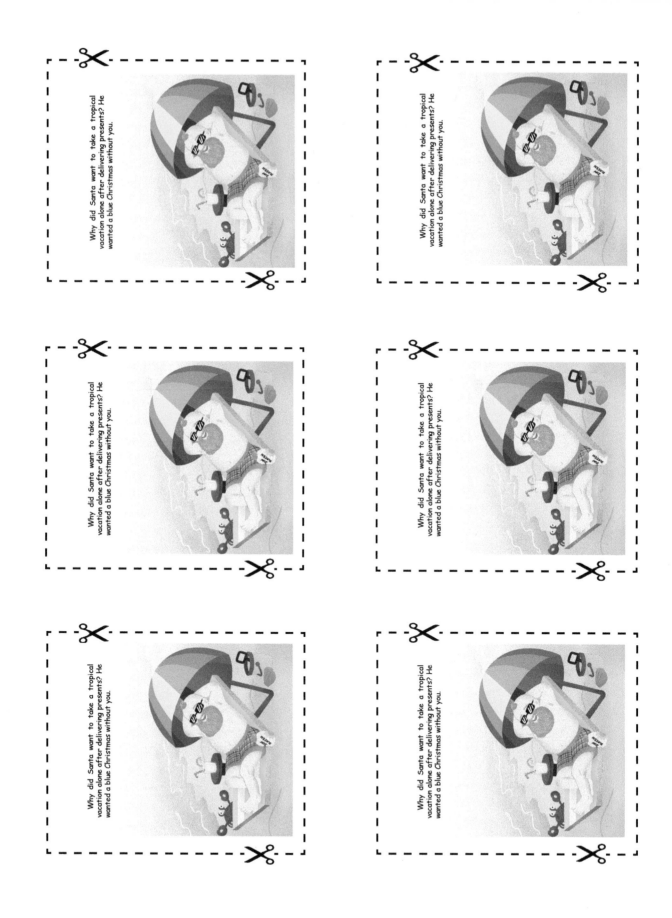

What did the polar bear say to Santa as she was giving him a bear hug because he gave her a present? "Grin and bear it."

What did the polar bear say to Santa as she was giving him a bear hug because he gave her a present? "Grin and bear it."

What did the polar bear say to Santa as she was giving him a bear hug because he gave her a present? "Grin and bear it."

What did the polar bear say to Santa as she was giving him a bear hug because he gave her a present? "Grin and bear it."

What did the polar bear say to Santa as she was giving him a bear hug because he gave her a present? "Grin and bear it."

What did the polar bear say to Santa as she was giving him a bear hug because he gave her a present? "Grin and bear it."

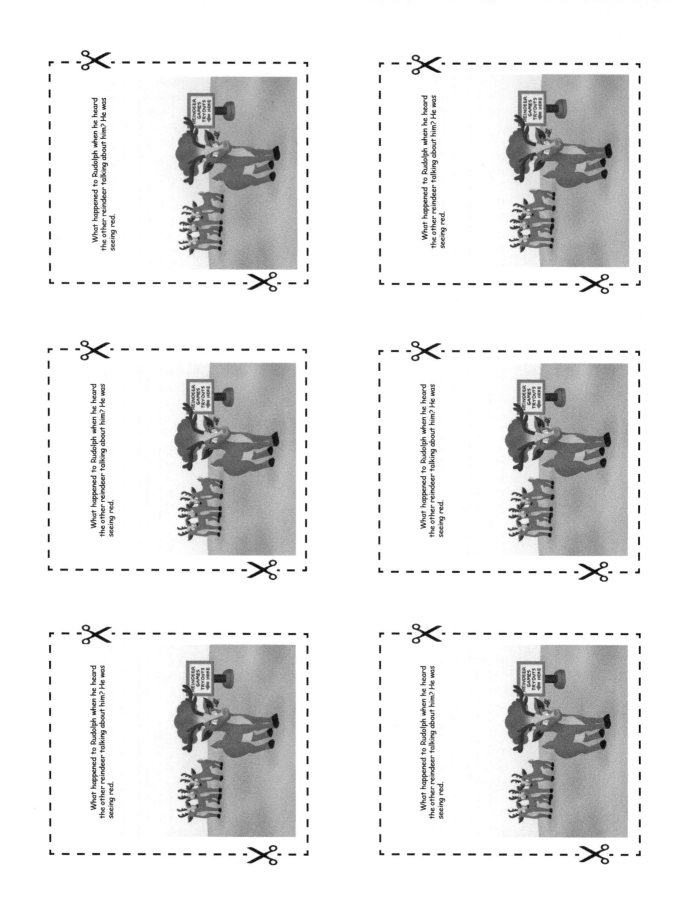

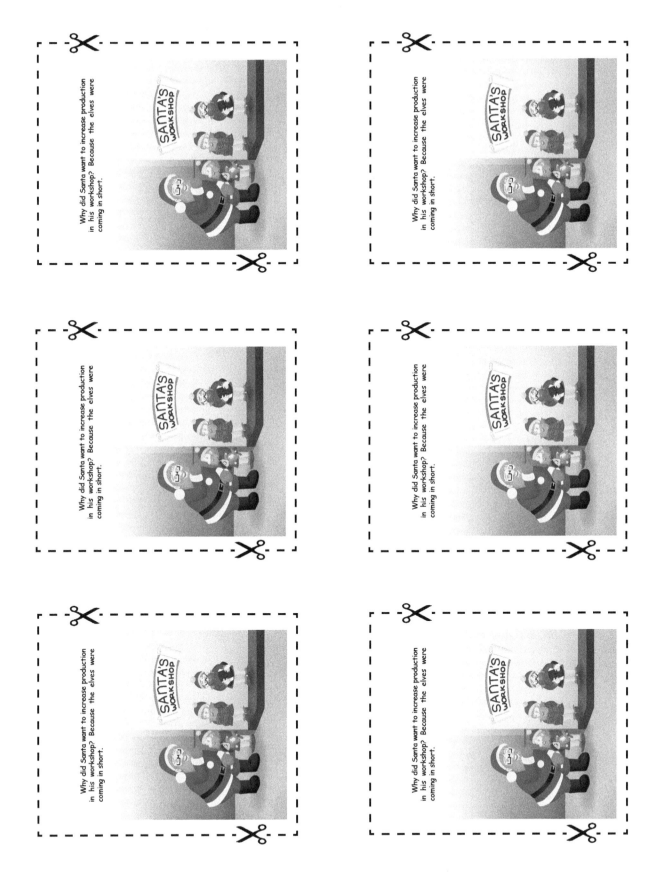

Why did Santa want to increase production in his workshop? Because the elves were coming in short.

Why did Santa want to increase production in his workshop? Because the elves were coming in short.

Why did Santa want to increase production in his workshop? Because the elves were coming in short.

Why did Santa want to increase production in his workshop? Because the elves were coming in short.

Why did Santa want to increase production in his workshop? Because the elves were coming in short.

Why did Santa want to increase production in his workshop? Because the elves were coming in short.

CPSIA information can be obtained
at www.ICGtesting.com
Printed in the USA
BVHW051337130921
616278BV00002B/36